MARK RYLANCE

Mark Rylance was born in England in 1960 and emigrated with his family to America in 1962. He lived in Connecticut until 1969 and then moved to Milwaukee, Wisconsin, where he lived until returning to London in 1978.

Mark trained at the Royal Academy of Dramatic Art (1978–80) under Hugh Cruttwell. The Glasgow Citizens Theatre gave him his first job in 1980, a year in repertoire, a trip to the carnival in Venice with Goldoni, and an Equity card.

He was the Artistic Director of Shakespeare's Globe Theatre (1996–2006). At the time of this publication, Mark's recent theatre work includes *Farinelli and the King* by Claire van Kampen; Countess Olivia in *Twelfth Night* and Richard III, directed by Tim Carroll; Johnny 'Rooster' Byron in *Jerusalem*, directed by Ian Rickson and written by Jez Butterworth. Recent film work includes Steven Spielberg's *The BFG* and *Bridge of Spies*; and for BBC Television, Flop in *Bing Bunny* and Thomas Cromwell in *Wolf Hall*, directed by Peter Kosminsky.

In 2007, he wrote his first play, *I Am Shakespeare*, produced by Greg Ripley Duggan and the Chichester Festival Theatre, directed by Matthew Warchus, and published in 2012 by Nick Hern Books.

Mark is an honorary bencher of the Middle Temple Hall in London; trustee of the Shakespearean Authorship Trust; an ambassador of Survival, the movement for tribal peoples; and a patron of Peace Direct, working for non-violent resolution of conflict.

He is married to Claire van Kampen, and a proud co-father with Chris van Kampen of Juliet and Nataasha.

LOUIS JENKINS

Louis Jenkins was born and raised in Oklahoma. In 1971, he moved with his wife Ann to Duluth, Minnesota, where he lived for forty-five years and spent most of that time complaining about the weather. His poems have been published in a number of literary magazines and anthologies, and he has seventeen collections of his poetry.

He was awarded two Bush Foundation Fellowships for poetry, a Loft-McKnight Fellowship, and was the 2000 George Morrison Award winner. He has read his poetry on *A Prairie Home Companion* and was a featured poet at the Geraldine R. Dodge Poetry Festival in 1996 and at the Aldeburgh Poetry Festival in the UK in 2007. He is at work on a new collection of prose poems to be published in 2017.

Mark Rylance & Louis Jenkins

NICE FISH

NICK HERN BOOKS
London
www.nickhernbooks.co.uk

A Nick Hern Book

Nice Fish first published in Great Britain as a paperback original in 2016 by Nick Hern Books Limited, The Glasshouse, 49a Goldhawk Road, London W12 8QP, by special arrangement with Grove Press, an imprint of Grove Atlantic, Inc., New York

Nice Fish copyright © 2016 Mark Rylance and Louis Jenkins
Introduction copyright © 2016 Mark Rylance and Louis Jenkins

Mark Rylance and Louis Jenkins have asserted their right to be identified as the authors of this work

Cover photograph of Mark Rylance and Jim Lichtscheidl: Richard Termine; artwork: aka.

Designed and typeset by Nick Hern Books, London
Printed in the UK by CPI Books (UK) Ltd

A CIP catalogue record for this book is available from the British Library

ISBN   978 1 84842 629 0

Poetry, Prose and Play

Louis Jenkins is a prose poet and here is his description of
a prose poem.

The Prose Poem

*The prose poem is not a real poem, of course. One of the major
differences is that the prose poet is incapable, either too lazy or
too stupid, of breaking the poem into lines. But all writing, even
the prose poem, involves a certain amount of skill, just the way
throwing a wad of paper, say, into a wastebasket at a distance
of twenty feet, requires a certain skill, a skill that, though it may
improve hand-eye coordination, does not lead necessarily to an
ability to play basketball. Still, it takes practice and thus gives
one a way to pass the time, chucking one paper after another at
the basket, while the teacher drones on about the poetry of
Tennyson.*

I suppose every play involves collaboration between
imagination and life, poetry and prose. When I was working on
this play, I used to sit on the bed of my friend James Hillman,
who was dying of cancer. James had studied the psyche all of
his life and we would chat about the emerging characters in this
play. One day he said to me, 'You know imagination exists. It is
not in us. We are in it.'

Autumn Leaves

*'And you call yourself a poet!' she said, laughing, walking
toward me. It was a woman I recognized, though I couldn't
remember her name. 'Here you are on the most beautiful day of
autumn... You should be writing a poem.' 'It's a difficult subject
to write about, the fall,' I said. 'Nevertheless,' she said, 'I saw
you drinking in the day, the pristine blue sky, the warm sunshine,*

*the brilliant leaves of the maples and birches rustled slightly by
the cool west wind which is the harbinger of winter.
I saw how you watched that maple leaf fall. I saw how you
picked it up and noted the flame color, touched here and there
with bits of gold and green and tiny black spots. I'm sure that
you saw in that leaf all the glory and pathos, the joy and
heartache of life on earth and yet you never touched pen to
paper.' 'Actually,' I said, 'most of what I write is simply made up,
not real at all.' 'So…?' she said.*

What is this play about? I don't know. I will be making sense of
it, word by word, as you are. We have read and re-read the
hundreds of poems Louis has written and selected poems and
passages to stitch together like an old American quilt of worn
beloved garments, each one bearing a pattern of history, an
experience. The Minnesota poet Robert Bly, who encouraged
Louis, heard the competing voices of a child and an adult in
Louis's first book. My experience of the Midwest of America
took place in my teenage, as I moved from childhood to
adulthood. Perhaps that early search for an identity that
encompassed both experiences drew me to these poems.

Jazz Poem

*I always wanted to write one of those Jazz poems. You know the
kind, where it's 3 a.m. in some incredibly smoky, out-of-the-way
little club in Chicago or New York, April 14, 1954 (it's always
good to give the date) and there are only a few sleepy people
left in the place, vacant tables with half-empty glasses,
overturned chairs… and then Bird or Leroy or someone plays
this incredible solo and it's like, it's like… well, you just should
have been there. The poet was there and you understand from
the poem that jazz is hip, intellectual, cool, but also earthy and
soulful, as the poet must be, as well, because he really digs this
stuff. Unfortunately, I grew up listening to rock and roll and
decidedly un-hip country music and it just doesn't work to say
you should have been in Gary Hofstadter's rec room, July 24,
1961, sipping a Pepsi, listening to Duane Eddy's latest album
and playing air guitar.*

Between 1969 and 1978, I lived primarily beside the crumbling
shores of Lake Michigan in one of the many crumbling

industrial cities of the North Midwest, Milwaukee, Wisconsin. Louis began his life in the dust of Oklahoma and followed his heart to Duluth, Minnesota, where he too has lived by a big lake, the deepest of all, Lake Superior. Perhaps it is our shared experience of these deep, dangerous and beautiful lakes bordering our cities that has brought us together. Perhaps it was just the cold, the snow and ice, burying every living thing under a white sheet until the spring wind arrived.

The Lake

Streets run straight downhill to the water. The lake brings the city to an end. It is there, always, changing the direction of my walks. Sometimes I go for days without coming near, catching only a glimpse through the trees: a sail, a white speck turning on the dark blue. Perhaps someone very old touched the back of my wrist, lightly, for only the briefest moment, or you said something to me. What was it? The waters close above my head suddenly without a sound.

But I think what really draws me to Louis is his ability to express an internal reality of what it feels like to be a human being through the description of an apparently external landscape. Perhaps James was right, 'The imagination is not within us, we are within it.'

Stone Arch, Natural Rock Formation

It is higher, more narrow, more treacherous than we imagined. And here we are in a spot where there's no going back, a point of no return. It has become too dangerous to continue as we have. We simply are not as sure-footed and nimble as we were when we started out. There's nothing to do but sit down, carefully, straddling the rock. Once seated, I'm going to turn slightly and hand the bag of groceries back to you. Then I'm going to scoot ahead a few inches and turn again. If you then lean forward carefully and hand me the bag you will be able to move ahead to the spot I previously occupied. It is a miserably slow process and we still have the problem of the steep descent on the other side. But if we are patient, my love, I believe we will arrive safely on the ground again a few yards from where we began.

I came up with the initial idea of making a play using the poetry of Louis Jenkins, but the words and story and images you will read here have arisen from collaborative play with my fellow actors, stage managers, director, designers, friends, all focusing on the life's work of Louis Jenkins. Now, of course, the play lives or dies in your imagination, and the final, essential, collaboration hopefully takes place. I hope our play returns you safely to the ground only a few yards from where you began.

Thanks

With special thanks for the collaboration of the cast and stage management of the 2013 Guthrie Theater production, the 2016 A.R.T. production, and Stuart Thompson's initial 2008 workshop at Playwright's Horizon on 42nd Street, New York. Sonia Friedman, and all her staff and angels at SFP, brought us to the Harold Pinter Theatre in London, and I will be eternally grateful.

Mark Rylance

Nice Fish was originally commissioned and produced by the Guthrie Theater, Minneapolis, Minnesota (Joe Dowling, Artistic Director) in 2013. It was further developed by the American Repertory Theater at Harvard University, Cambridge, Massachusetts (Diane Paulus, Artistic Director; Diane Borger, Producer), and subsequently transferred to St Ann's Warehouse, Brooklyn, New York, on 14 February 2016. The play received its UK premiere at the Harold Pinter Theatre, London on 15 November 2016.

The West End cast was as follows:

WAYNE	Raye Birk
FLO	Kayli Carter
THE DNR MAN	Bob Davis
ERIK	Jim Lichtscheidl
RON	Mark Rylance
PUPPETEER	Mohsen Nouri

Director	Claire van Kampen
Set	Todd Rosenthal
Costume	Ilona Somogyi
Lighting	Japhy Weideman
Sound	Scott W. Edwards
Original Music	Claire van Kampen
Casting	Jim Carnahan CSA
Puppetry	Sarah Wright

The American Repertory Theater production was produced in the West End by Sonia Friedman Productions in association with 1001 Nights Productions, Paula Marie Black, Rupert Gavin, Tulchin Bartner Productions, Brian Zeilinger.

At the Guthrie Theater, Wayne was played by Chris Carlson, Flo by Emily Swallow, and Wainwright by Tyson Forbes.

At the American Repertory Theater, Wayne was played by Louis Jenkins.

The original 2008 workshop production at Playwright's Horizons, New York, was performed by Matthew Cowles and Mark Rylance.

Dedicated

to

Nataasha

James Hillman and Matthew Cowles

Characters

ERIK, *married. Unemployed. An ice-fishing enthusiast. Around fifty in age. Old college friend of Ron's. From Minnesota.*

RON, *single. Employed. Knows little about ice fishing. Around fifty in age. Old college friend of Erik's. From Wisconsin.*

FLO *or* FLORENCE, *an independent woman. Wayne's granddaughter.*

WAYNE, *a devoted spear fisherman. A widower, retired, mid-sixties to mid-seventies in age, Flo's grandfather.*

THE DNR MAN, *an officer from the Minnesota Department of Natural Resources (DNR).*

This text went to press before the end of rehearsals and so may differ slightly from the play as performed.

ACT ONE

Preset and Scene One

The Ice Fisherman

A frozen lake somewhere in Northern Minnesota.

Late winter. Early spring.

The last day of ice-fishing season.

Early morning.

Upstage, a high wall of white cloud, divisible from the snowy white ice of the lake only by a very distant shoreline of spruce trees and bare poplars, which disappears from stage right into the far horizon center stage.

Only a few miniature brightly painted ice-fishing huts are visible on the ice in front of the distant shoreline. Perhaps a miniature truck pulls an ice house off of the ice. The shore looks unpopulated. We are far north.

We hear the sound of the ice booming as it shifts and cracks. The wind. Distant snowmobiles. Perhaps we hear, drifting across the ice, a little of 'The Calle Schewen Waltz' played by Mel Brenden and the Minnesota Scandinavian Ensemble.

A train passes slowly along the shoreline. We see its lights and hear its whistle.

Mid-stage, we see a man in black ice fishing as described in the following poem.

All distant characters are portrayed by puppets operated from below.

We hear the voice of Louis Jenkins, or WAYNE.

WAYNE (*off*). From here he appears as a black spot, one of the shadows that today has found it necessary to assume solid form. Along with the black jut of shoreline far to the left, he is the only break in the undifferentiated gray of ice and overcast sky.

Here is a man going jiggidy-jig-jig in a black hole. Depth and the current are of only incidental interest to him. He's after something big, something down there that is pure need, something that, had it the wherewithal, would swallow him whole.

Right now nothing is happening. The fisherman stands and straightens, back to the wind. He stays out on the ice all day.

Blackout.

Scene Two

A Strike Master Hand-held Ice Auger

Lights up.

Very early morning.

A beautiful morning sky at back.

Mid-stage left, apparently a hundred yards away, a seemingly abandoned ice house has appeared. It has a chimney and one side of it has sunk into the ice a foot or so and refrozen. It has a door on the stage-right side. Snow has drifted up over it and around it, covering a sofa that is on the downstage side but leaving visible a black barbecue stove, on the stage-left side. Underneath the snow covering one can see patches of color where the front of the hut has been painted with a beach scene of palm trees, sun and sand. There is a small window in the downstage side.

There are two other more conventional huts in the far distance before you get to the shore.

Offstage right, always unseen to the audience, WAYNE's spear-fishing house and ERIK's truck will be referred to.

Downstage right we see RON, or a bundle of winter clothes inside of which, somewhere, is RON. He is drilling a hole in the ice by hand with a Strike Master hand-held ice auger. Standing behind him, holding some fishing equipment and watching, we see ERIK.

A few moments.

Blackout.

Scene Three

A Strike Master Gas-powered Ice Auger

In the darkness, we hear the sound of the gas-powered auger start up.

Lights up.

ERIK, *similarly dressed for the intense cold, is drilling a second hole in the ice with a Strike Master gas-powered auger.* RON, *collapsed on the ice with his hand-held auger, watches, exhausted.*

Blackout.

Scene Four

In Just a Little Closer

Lights up.

ERIK *places his underwater camera, radar, and bucket with fishing poles next to his freshly drilled fishing hole. His is the stage-left hole. He opens his tackle box.*

RON *is seated on one of two five-gallon buckets that have appeared, unpacking his new sunglasses.*

It is quite cold.

ERIK. I've spent a great deal of my life fretting over things that most people wouldn't waste their time on. Trying to explain something I haven't a clue about. It's given me that worried look, that wide-eyed, staring look. The look that wild animals sometimes have, deer for instance, trying to make sense of the situation: 'What is that?' Motionless, transfixed. The same look that's on the face of this fishing lure. Stupidity? Terror? What is the right bait for these conditions? High stratus clouds, maybe snow later. It's all a trick anyway. What is this thing supposed to be? A minnow? A bug? Gaudy paint and hooks all over. It's like bleached-blond hair and bright-red lipstick. Nobody really believes it. There isn't a way in the world I'd bite on that thing.

RON. I might swim in just a little closer.

Blackout.

Scene Five

The Back Country

Lights up.

RON approaches from offstage right, as if he is coming from the offstage truck, carrying his blue chair, and wheeling a red-and-white cooler.

He is wearing fancy new sunglasses, label still attached, over the brow of his hat.

ERIK is looking at the gear on a sled, which has also appeared, and setting up his fishing technology, radar, underwater camera, etc.

RON speaks with the audience.

RON. When you are in town, wearing some kind of uniform is helpful, policeman, priest, et cetera. Driving a tank is very impressive, or a car with official lettering on the side. If that isn't to your taste, you could join the revolution, wear an armband, carry a home-made flag tied to a broom handle, or a placard bearing an incendiary slogan. At the very least, you should wear a suit and carry a briefcase and a cellphone, or wear a team jacket and a baseball cap and carry a cellphone. If you go into the woods, the back country, someplace past all human habitation, it is a good idea to wear orange and carry a gun, or, depending on the season, carry a fishing pole, or a camera with a big lens. Otherwise, it might appear that you have no idea what you are doing, that you are merely wandering the earth, no particular reason for being here, no particular place to go.

RON accidentally drops his cellphone into the fishing hole. When he looks down to see what has happened, his sunglasses also fall into the hole.

He looks at ERIK.

Blackout.

Scene Six

Everything You Have is Lost

Lights up.

RON *is looking into the fishing hole for his phone.*

ERIK *is returning from downstage left where he has just drilled a third hole with the gas-powered auger.*

RON *looks up and listens to* ERIK *as he speaks.*

ERIK. In the morning, after I dressed, I looked for my wristwatch on the nightstand and discovered that it was missing. I looked in the drawer and on the floor, under the bed. It was nowhere to be seen. I looked in the bathroom, checked the pockets of my jacket, my pants. I looked downstairs in the kitchen, the living room. I went out to check the car. I went to the basement and looked through the laundry. I went back upstairs and looked everywhere again.

RON unfolds his blue fishing chair to sit on. Without stopping speaking ERIK *takes it from him, folding it back up and placing a five-gallon bucket for* RON *to sit on instead of the chair.* RON *sits down.* ERIK *gives him a fishing pole and puts bait on it for him.*

I said, 'Have you seen my watch?' to my wife, my children. 'I'm sure I left it on the nightstand.' I became obsessed with finding the watch. I removed all the drawers from the dresser one by one, emptying their contents on to the bedroom floor. Impossible. Someone must have come in the night and taken it. A watch thief, who with great stealth and cunning, disdaining silverware, jewelry, cameras, fine art, money, had made his way to the bedside and stolen my Timex wristwatch. Perhaps my wife has, for years, been harboring some secret grudge and finally, unable to bear it any longer, took revenge by flushing my watch down the toilet. Maybe my seven-year-old is supporting a drug habit. One thing is certain: nothing, nothing was the way I thought it was.

RON. Yeah, or you've lost something, your car keys, or your watch and you have searched for what seems like hours. But then suddenly it appears, right there on the table, not two feet away.

ERIK. 'If it was a snake it would have bit you,' Mother said.

RON. And, that's what you remember, a phrase, an old saying. My sister said, 'Grandma told me, "Never wear horizontal stripes, they make you look fat." That's one of the few things I remember about Grandma.'

ERIK. Or the words disappear and an image remains. I was getting a lecture from my parents about riding my tricycle all the way downtown. I don't remember anything they said. I remember looking out the window, it was just dark, and a block away a man wearing a white shirt and a tie passed under the streetlight and vanished into the night. That's all. Out of a lifetime, a few words, a few pictures, and everything you have lost is lurking there in the dark, poised to strike.

RON. It's so easy to lose track of things. A screwdriver, for instance. 'Where did I put that? I had it in my hand just a minute ago.' You wander vaguely from room to room, having forgotten, by now, what you were looking for, staring into the refrigerator, the bathroom mirror... 'I really could use a shave...'

Blackout.

Scene Seven

Old Friends

Lights up.

Later.

They are fishing.

RON. There's a game we play,

RON *and* ERIK. not a game exactly,

ERIK *and* RON. a sort of call-and-response.

ERIK. It's one of the pleasures of living for a long time in a fairly small place.

RON. You know, they lived over by Plett's Grocery.

ERIK. Where that bank is now?

RON. That's right.

ERIK. Plett's, I'd almost forgotten. Do you remember where Ward's was?

RON. Didn't they tear it down to build the Holiday Mall?

ERIK. Yes.

RON. I remember. The Holiday Mall.

ERIK. It works for people, too. Remember the guy who came to all the art exhibit openings?

RON. The guy with the hat?

ERIK. Yeah, he came for the free food and drinks.

RON. Right. And there was the guy with the pipe and the tweed jacket...

ERIK. ... who always said hello to everyone

RON. because he wasn't sure who he actually knew.

ERIK. Oh, yes!

RON. It's like the words to an old song,

ERIK. la, la, la,

RON. some of which you remember.

ERIK. And after we have gone someone will say,

RON. 'Oh him.

ERIK. I thought he was still around.

RON. I used to see him everywhere, only,

ERIK. all this time, I thought he was someone else.'

Blackout.

Scene Eight

How Do You Tell a Wolf from a Dog?

A dog barks fiercely in the distance.

Lights up.

ERIK *is fishing.*

RON *appears to have rushed on from stage left, out of breath.*

RON. How do you tell a wolf from a dog?

ERIC. A wolf carries his head down, tail down. He has a look of preoccupation, or worry, you might think. He has a family to support. He probably has a couple of broken ribs from trying to bring down a moose. He's not getting workman's comp, either, and no praise for his efforts. The wolf looks unemployed, flat broke.

Pause.

On the other hand, a dog of similar features, a husky or a malamute, has his head up, ears up, looks attentive, self-confident, cheerful and obedient. He is fully employed with an eye toward promotion. He carries his tail high, like a banner. He's part of a big organization and has the title of 'man's best friend'.

Blackout.

Scene Nine

Time Marches On

Lights up.

ERIK *and* RON *standing together, looking out.*

ERIK *is drinking coffee.* RON *is having a beer.*

RON. How quickly the days are passing,

ERIK. Crazy Days,

RON. Wrong Days in Wright,

ERIK. Rutabaga Days,

RON. Duck Days, Red Flannel Days. Gone the Black Fly Festival,

ERIC. the Eelpout Festival,

RON. Finn Fest, the Carnivore's Ball, the Five-Mile-Long Rummage Sale; all have passed.

ERIC. What has passed is forever lost.

RON. Modern Dance on the Bridge Abutment, the Hardanger Fiddle Association of America Meeting, the Polka Mass, 'O, lost and by the wind grieved...', the Inline Skate Marathon, the Jet Ski Grand Prix...

ERIC. What is past is as though it never was.

ERIK *goes back to fishing alone.*

RON. The Battle of the Bands, the Polar Bear Plunge, the Monster Truck Challenge... Being mostly water as we are, it's not so bad living in a cold climate like this one. It gives you a certain solidity. Cold feet, the icy handshake, the cold shoulder, the frozen countenance, shouldn't be thought of as ill will but as a kind of preservation.

RON *drops his empty beer can down the stage-left ice hole.*

But everyone gets a little crazy when it's very cold for several weeks. Some people go in for compulsive house-cleaning, others read, read everything: milk cartons, shipping labels... We eat too much. We sleep a lot too. Once, during a cold spell, I slept for three days and when I woke I drank a gallon and a half of coffee. Sometimes we drive nails with a frozen banana. Sometimes we just watch the numbers on the gas and the electric meters go spinning by. There's just no end to the fun.

Blackout.

Scene Ten

A World Beyond My Imagining

Lights up.

RON *is sitting opening a big can of beer and trying to fish again.*

ERIK *is fishing.*

While ERIK *speaks* RON *falls asleep.*

ERIK. I returned to my ancestral home last year. We came to
    a beautiful little farm. From photos I'd seen I knew this was
    the place. It was nearly midsummer, the trees and grass, lush
    green. When we arrived the family was gathered at a table on
    the lawn for coffee and fresh strawberries. Introductions were
    made all around, Grandpa Sven, Lars-Olaf and Marie, Erik and
    Gudren, Cousin Inge and her two children... It made me think
    of a Carl Larsson painting. But, the Swedes are very up to
    date, Lars-Olaf was an engineer for Volvo. They all spoke
    perfect English, except for Grandpa, and there was a great deal
    of laughter over my attempts at Swedish. We stayed for a long
    time laughing and talking. I felt a wonderful kinship. It seemed
    to me that I had known these people all my life, they even
    looked like family back in the States. But as it turned out we
    had come to the wrong farm. Lars-Olaf said, 'I think I know
    your people, they live about three miles from here. If you like
    I could give them a call.' I said that no, it wasn't necessary, this
    was close enough.

ERIK *notices that* RON *has fallen asleep.*

He feels a bite on his line and reels in RON's *empty beer can.*

Ron! Ron!

RON. Yeah, I know what you mean, Swedish girls. Thanks I've
    got one. The other morning at the mall I passed a young
    Swedish girl that was wearing a very tight orange T-shirt
    with FLORIDA printed on the front in large white letters.
    Naturally I thought of citrus fruit.

I have never been to Florida but I know there are drug dealers,
    red tide, walking catfish, Republicans, Disney World,

alligators, hanging chads... Still, the citrus fruit is very good this time of year and when I peel an orange and look out the window at the snow and the rough spruce trees it seems like a miracle. One taste and I know there is a world beyond my imagining. It's impossible, like love, yet it really exists.

Blackout.

Scene Eleven

Silence

Lights up.

RON *and* ERIK *are sitting fishing.*

They have run out of things to say.

Blackout.

Scene Twelve

The Singing Fish

In the darkness, the sound of strange singing.

Lights up.

ERIK *is trying to fish.*

RON *stands near holding a singing fish in its box. He dances to the music and draws* ERIK*'s attention to the end of the song when the fish turns out and opens its mouth wide.*

Blackout.

Scene Thirteen

The Snowman

Lights up.

RON *has made a snowman.*

RON. Hey, Erik, what would a snowman say if he could talk?

'I don't have the top hat like my ancestors… well, my
predecessors, had. No, I've got a mad bomber hat.'

RON *puts his own hat on the snowman's head. He gets lures
and bobs from* ERIK*'s tackle box to decorate the snowman.*
ERIK *tries to resist.*

'Quite trendy, I think. I've had to give up the pipe and
I never drink. Still, I've got a big smile for everyone. I'm
a traditionalist. I like the old songs, "White Christmas",
"Ain't Misbehavin' "", "Don't Get Around Much Anymore",
songs like that. But I try to stay up to date, try to be aware of
what's happening. I'm very concerned about global warming
for instance, but it's difficult in my field to get any real
information. And what can I do?

Not that I'm complaining. I like it here; I feel at home, very
much a part of my environment. It does get lonely at times
though, there are so very few women in these parts, and I'm
not the best-looking guy around, with my strange build and
very odd nose. Sometimes I think they put my nose in the
wrong place.'

ERIK *takes the head of the snowman and puts it in a bucket.*
RON *places his own head on the remaining body of the
snowman.*

'Still, I have always hoped that someone would come along,
someone who would melt in my arms. A woman with whom
I could become one. You wouldn't guess it to look at me but
I'm a romantic. But it's getting rather late in the season for
me. So, I'm inclined just to drift…'

RON *pretends to drift and melt as the snowman.*

'I don't have any problems getting through the night; it's the
days that are so long and difficult now that spring is coming.

Oh, spring is so beautiful with the new buds on the trees and the bright sunshine, but it's such a melancholy season. It causes one to reflect... Oh, but here I go, running off at the mouth again.'

Blackout.

Scene Fourteen

The Man from the Department of Natural Resources

Lights up.

The DNR MAN *is standing there.*

The snowman has gone.

RON *is making a snow angel, downstage left.*

ERIK *is fishing.*

DNR. That your vehicle?

RON. A-huh.

DNR. Is that your fish house?

RON. No.

DNR. You know that has to be off the ice by midnight tomorrow?

RON. It isn't my house.

DNR. Whose is it then?

RON. No idea.

DNR. Is that a spear-fishing set-up?

RON. What?

DNR. Is that a dark house for spear fishing?

RON. Where?

DNR. Over there behind your vehicle.

RON. Don't know.

DNR. Spear fishing has been prohibited on these waters since the end of February.

RON. Okay.

DNR. All shelters must be off the ice no later than midnight of the specified closing date and on this lake that date is tomorrow, March 18th. That only leaves you thirty-eight hours to get these off the ice.

RON. They aren't mine.

DNR. Mmm-hmm. Name on the house says Wayne Johnson. That you?

RON. No it is not.

DNR. The regulations state that if shelters are not removed on the specified date, owners will be prosecuted, and the structure and contents may be confiscated and removed, or destroyed by a conservation officer.

You got a fishing license?

ERIK *shows him his own license.*

ERIK. He's not fishing.

DNR. He's not fishing. This says Mr Elwin Erik Johnson. That you?

ERIK. Yes.

RON. Elwin?

DNR. Not Wayne?

ERIK. Nope.

RON. Your name's Elwin?

ERIK. Yeah.

DNR. Wayne a relative?

ERIK. No. I don't know Wayne Johnson, I never heard of Wayne Johnson.

DNR. Spear fishing is illegal on these waters now, Mr Johnson.

ERIK. I know.

DNR. You mind if I inspect your equipment?

The DNR MAN *begins to look through* ERIK*'s tackle box.*

He's going to need a license.

ERIK. He's not fishing.

RON. Okay. I'll get a license. I don't mind, Erik. How much are they?

DNR. I'm going to have to confiscate this. An Alabama umbrella rig is not legal in Minnesota waters.

He puts it in his pocket.

ERIK. If you remove all the hooks but one, it is.

The DNR MAN *looks in his booklet of regulations and replaces the rig.*

DNR. These batteries have got mercury in them.

He puts them in his pocket.

ERIK. They're for my flashlight.

The DNR MAN *takes them out of his pocket and gives them back to* ERIK.

DNR. Would you store them separately from your tackle, Wayne, I mean Mr Johnson.

A resident individual (annual) fishing license, Code one-one-one, costs twenty-two dollars.

ERIK. There's only thirty-eight hours left.

DNR. A resident seventy-two-hour individual fishing license, code one-forty, will cost you twelve dollars. In the event the angler purchases an annual individual fishing license later in the same license year, the cost of the seventy-two-hour license will apply towards the purchase of the annual fishing license.

RON. If I purchase a resident seventy-two-hour individual fishing license, code one-forty, now for twelve dollars, and then purchase a resident individual annual fishing license, code one...

DNR. Eleven.

RON. Eleven, for twenty-four dollars...

DNR. Twenty-two dollars.

RON. Twenty-two dollars... after the seventy-two hours has expired, will the cost of the seventy-two-hour resident individual fishing license apply towards the purchase of the resident individual annual fishing license next year?

DNR. No.

RON. Okay.

DNR. Have you got a driver's license?

RON. Sure.

> RON *shows him his license*.

DNR. You're a non-resident.

RON. No I'm not. I'm an American.

DNR. This is a Wisconsin driver's license.

ERIK. How much is a non-resident one-day fishing license?

DNR. A non-resident seventy-two-hour individual fishing license, code one-three-nine, will cost you twenty-four dollars.

ERIK. We're only here today.

DNR. Have you got your Annual Great Lakes Trout and Walleye Stamp Privilege?

RON. What's that?

DNR. The ten-dollar trout stamp is required in addition to your fishing license to fish designated trout streams, trout lakes and the big lake. For an extra seventy-five cents you can get an actual trout or walleye pictorial stamp, a stunning reproduction of an award-winning oil painting by a talented Minnesota artist.

RON. Are they collectable?

ERIK. Okay okay. We'll take a non-resident seventy-two-hour individual license for him and I'll have the trout for ten dollars.

RON. Can I have some fries with that?

DNR. That'll cost you thirty-four dollars.

> ERIK *gets out his phone and starts to purchase a license online*.

RON. I've got this, Erik.

> RON *has got his money out*.

DNR. I don't accept cash. You can pay online, on a smartphone, computer, tablet, or at www.dnr.state.mn.us/licenses, or call 1-888-MN-LICEN (665-4236). Have you got a phone?

RON *looks at his ice-fishing hole.*

As he speaks he offers cash to the officer as a bribe.

RON. Sure. Listen, sir, can I have a word? I lost my phone down that ice hole and I don't want to ask my buddy to pay for me. I'm not a fisherman. I don't know the first thing about fishing. I don't even like the outdoors. There's only one day left, so could we just let this whole thing slide, just this once. I mean, are there any other options?

The DNR MAN *gets out his pad and starts to make out a ticket.*

What are you doing?

DNR. The fine for a non-resident who is illegally fishing in Minnesota waters, a hundred and eighty-five dollars. The fine for your buddy for failure to possess a trout stamp and attempted bribery, let me see what the options are here...

ERIK *shows the* DNR MAN *his phone.*

ERIK. I gotcha, Ron.

DNR. I'd recommend you make a hole next to your vehicle and if the water starts to overflow the top of the hole, the ice is sinking and it's time to move the vehicle.

RON. The ice is sinking?

DNR. There's no such thing as a hundred-per-cent safe ice.

RON. What do I do if I break through?

DNR. If you break through? Remain calm. Turn in the direction you came from. That's probably the strongest ice. Dig your picks or ice claws into the ice and while vigorously kicking your legs, pull yourself on to the surface of the ice. Distribute your weight, to avoid breaking through again, by rolling away from the area of weakest ice. Get to shelter, heat, warm dry clothing and warm, non-alcoholic and non-caffeinated drinks.

RON *moves over to* ERIK, *looking offstage to the truck.*

What are you fellas doing so far out here anyway?

ERIK. Bowling.

DNR. Okay, guys, do me a favor. Get these shelters off the ice by midnight tomorrow...

The DNR MAN *turns and speaks directly with the audience.*

Because of my extraordinary correctness and sensitivity of late I have been elevated to the status of Temporary Minor Saint (secular). The position comes with a commendation praising my (quote) 'uncharacteristic reticence tantamount to sagacity' (end quote). This means that my entire being is now suffused with a pale radiance somewhat like the light from a small fluorescent bulb, the light on a kitchen range perhaps, only not quite so bright, and that instead of walking I now float at an altitude of approximately three inches above the ground. I move to the left or right by inclining my head and upper body in the appropriate direction. It's a less-than-perfect condition. The light keeps my wife awake at night and though the added height is beneficial, moving about in a crowd presents difficulties. My forward speed seems to be fixed and, though slow, is quite tricky to stop. I lean back but momentum carries me forward like a boat. Suddenly turning my head can send me veering into the person next to me or into a wall. In order to remain in one place I've found it necessary to attach cords to my belt on one end and to various solid objects around the room on the other. These days I take my meals standing up, tethered like the *Hindenburg*.

Blackout.

Scene Fifteen

The Pop-up Ice House

The ice cracks and booms. A distant snowmobile.

Lights up.

Brighter.

Clouds have cleared.

ERIK *is setting up the pop-up tent, with occasional and distracted help from* RON, *who is drinking a beer and setting up his chair when the lights come up.*

RON. Look at that, Erik. Just look at it. The sky is the exact color of Mary Beth Anderson's eyes.

ERIK. Ron.

RON. Beautiful, perfect. Perfect hair and perfect teeth. It always seemed that she knew exactly what she wanted and where she was going, that she had planned her life in detail. I liked her immediately, her blue eyes, the way she listened, as if what I said was fascinating, the easy, natural way she laughed at all my jokes. Her rather conventional good looks and dress belied her intelligence. We had things in common, an interest in art and humanism. She talked about the problems of coffee growers in Central America. I listened, but I also thought about kissing her on the neck, where her blond hair curled just behind her ear.

RON *tries to help by popping the tent inside out and accidentally collapsing it again. While* ERIK *is distracted inside the collapsed tent:*

I thought about other things, too. Mostly we laughed. Then she was silent. She looked at me. I saw that her eyes were gray, not blue. She was serious.

ERIK *emerges from the tent, takes the empty tent bag from* RON *and returns to his fishing hole.* RON *follows him.*

She said, 'Ron, this has gone too far in too short a time. I feel as though I'm being smothered. I have no time to myself anymore. I feel like you are always there. And I can't even so much as speak to another man…' 'What are you talking about?' I said, 'We only met an hour ago!'

Blackout.

Scene Sixteen

A New View of the World

Lights up.

Later, midday, lunchtime.

RON *has been talking about his troubles with women for some time.*

ERIK *is still trying to fish.*

RON. There was a young couple in the parking lot, kissing. Not just kissing, they looked as though they might eat each other up, kissing, nibbling, biting, mouths wide open, play-fighting like young dogs, wrapped around each other like snakes. I remember that, sort of, that hunger, that passionate intensity. And I get a kind of nostalgic craving for it, in the way that I get a craving, occasionally, for the food of my childhood.

RON *opens the cooler and takes out and makes his lunch as he describes.*

Baloney on white bread, for instance: one slice of white bread with mustard or Miracle Whip ('New Look, Same Great Taste') or ketchup – not ketchup, one has to draw the line somewhere – and one slice of baloney. It had a nice symmetry to it, the circle of baloney on the rectangle of bread. Then you folded the bread and baloney in the middle and took a bite out of the very *center* of the folded side.

RON *takes a bite out of the sandwich as he describes.*

When you unfolded the sandwich you had a hole, a circle in the center of the bread-and-baloney frame, a window, a porthole from which you could get a new view of the world.

He looks through the hole he has made in his piece of bread.

ERIK *moves away from* RON, *speaking with himself/the audience.*

ERIK. Some days are so sad nothing will help, when love has gone, when the sunshine and clear sky only tease and mock you. Those days you feel like running away, going where no

one knows your name. Like slinging the old Gibson over
your shoulder and travelling the narrow road to the north
where the gray sky fits your mood and the cold wind blows
a different kind of trouble. Nothing up there but mosquito-
infested swamp, ten thousand acres of hummocky muck,
a thicket of alder and dogwood, a twisted tangle of
complications where not even Hemingway would fish. But
somebody, someday soon, somebody will come and put up
a bed and breakfast and a gourmet coffee shop. There is only
one true wilderness left to explore, those vast empty spaces
in your head.

The ice booms and cracks. The wind blows.

*Sounds of nature. Migrating birds overhead. Perhaps
a distant train.*

Nature is speaking with ERIK. *This is what he came for.*

Blackout.

Scene Seventeen

Those Vast Empty Spaces in Your Head

Lights up.

ERIK *is standing on his own.* RON *is offstage sitting in the truck.*

We hear its engine running.

We hear rock music blaring loud inside the truck.

ERIK. Ron. RON! RON! TURN OFF THE TRUCK! YOU'RE WASTING FUEL! YOU'RE DISTURBING THE FISH! THE FISH, RON!

ERIK *gestures and mimes his meaning.*

We hear the music louder as RON *opens the truck door.*

RON. WHAT?

ERIK. TURN OFF THE MUSIC, RON.

RON. WHAT?

ERIK. TURN OFF THE MUSIC, RON.

The music stops.

YOU'RE DISTURBING THE FISH! THE FISH, RON! THE VIBRATIONS ARE DRIVING THEM AWAY! TURN OFF THE TRUCK! TURN IT OFF! YOU'RE WASTING FUEL!

RON. I'm cold.

ERIK. TURN OFF THE TRUCK! TURN IT OFF! We're meant to be fishing…

The truck stops. The door slams shut.

ERIK *goes back to fishing.*

After a moment the music goes on again, loud inside the truck.

ERIK *picks up the singing fish and goes to rip it out of its box.*

Blackout.

Scene Eighteen

Spring Wind

The sound of strong wind in the blackout.

Lights up.

The wind has picked up strong now. The pop-up tent shakes.

RON *is sitting inside looking out through the window flap.*

ERIK *is sitting at his ice hole, fishing, and muttering to himself, furiously.*

The smashed singing fish is at his feet.

A Vikings umbrella blows across the stage above their heads.

RON *has raised his voice above the wind.*

RON. The spring wind comes through and knocks over trash cans and trees. It has something to do with warm fronts and cold fronts, I think, or with high and low pressure systems, things that I don't really understand and that aren't really an explanation anyway. Ultimately the spring wind is the result of some relationship between the earth and the sun that may not be all that healthy, after all. The wind comes in a big huff, slams doors, pushes things around and kicks up the dirt. The big bully spring wind comes through on its way nowhere and, ha ha! We love it.

The wind lifts the pop-up ice house and it blows off into the stage-left wings.

Blackout.

and

Lights up.

RON *and* ERIK *are trying to hold on to each other in the middle of the stage.*

Blackout.

and

Lights up.

RON *and* ERIK *are extended horizontally on the cooler and a bucket, legs stretched out in the wind, holding on to things by their fishing holes.* RON *holds on to his folded chair, which the wind blows away stage right. If possible, the snow covering the sauna house blows off, revealing a naive painting of palm trees and a beach scene.*

Blackout.

ACT TWO

Scene One

Flo

Lights up.

The wind has calmed.

RON *is holding the broken singing fish.* ERIK *is fishing again. They do not seem together.*

The door of the sauna ice house is open.

A large cloud of steam billows out from the sauna within.

A puppet of FLO *is standing just outside the door of the sauna house, brushing her hair. She turns and looks at the fishermen.*

Blackout.

and

Lights up.

FLO *herself is standing down by the stage-left fishing hole.*

She is holding a copy of Moby Dick *and a camera.*

ERIK *and* RON *are looking at her.*

Greetings have already been exchanged.

FLO. It seems like starfish don't do anything, you know, but actually they move along at a rate of about sixty feet per hour. A starfish will eat anything that moves slower than it does, which excludes a great number of dishes from its diet. A starfish is all arms and appetite; it has no brain, yet in spite of this, time-lapse photography has shown that the starfish maintains an active social life. So in these regards the starfish is like many people you know.

RON. There aren't any starfish down there or Erik would have caught one.

ERIK. There aren't any starfish down there.

FLO. No. No starfish down there.

RON. How come your hair's all wet?

FLO. I fell asleep in the sauna.

RON. In the sauna? Where?

FLO *points to her sauna hut.*

That's your ice house?

ERIK. You got a sauna in there?

FLO. Yea. Isn't that cool. We could heat it up again, if we got some more propane gas from my Grandpa Wayne's dark house over there. Sweating is the only way our bodies get rid of heavy metals.

Pause.

When I was a child I had a pair of canaries in a cage in my room. I had the idea that I would raise and sell canaries. You guys kinda reminded me of them when I saw you.

ERIK. Canaries.

FLO. Yea they had colored coats just like yours, red and yellow and orange. One of them had an orange head just like yours. I mean like your hat.

RON. It's so I don't get lost in a white-out.

FLO. I remember how the female canary ignored the male, but chirped plaintively to a mockingbird that sang outside my window all summer long.

RON. Well, we know that birds' singing has to do with territory and breeding rights.

ERIK. We do?

RON. Sure. I read it.

ERIK. You read it. Where?

RON. *National Geographic. National Enquirer.* One of those... magazines... nature magazines. Male birds sing to attract females...

FLO. and warn away other males.

RON. That's right. Their songs can include threat and intimidation, and perhaps, in the more complicated songs...

ERIK. the threat of legal action?

RON. It's the grim business of earning a living in a grim world, Erik.

FLO. Each song has its own subtle sound, the idiosyncrasies of its singer.

It turns out, though, that the females don't really value innovation and invention and generally mate with males that sing the most ordinary, traditional tune.

RON. You see, Erik.

FLO. There is always though, some poor sap, some melodious bachelor, that doesn't get it, sitting alone on his branch practicing and polishing his peculiar version until it flows smoothly as water through the streambed, a happy song that fills us with joy on this first warm day of the year.

ERIK. Hey, Ron, did you know, when the morning comes that you don't wake up, what remains of your life goes on as some kind of electromagnetic energy. There's a slight chance you might appear on someone's screen as a dot. Face it. You are a blip or a ping, part of the background noise, the residue of the Big Bang. You remember the Big Bang, don't you, Ron? You were about twenty-six years old, driving a brand new red-and-white Chevy convertible, with that beautiful blond girl at your side, Charlene, was her name. You had a case of beer on ice in the back, cruising down Highway number 7 on a summer afternoon and then you parked near Loon Lake just as the moon began to rise. Way back then you said to yourself, 'Boy, it doesn't get any better than this,' and you were right.

RON. You don't know what you're talking about.

FLO. It's true, it doesn't get any better than this.

ERIK. You see, Ron.

RON. So, what was it like when you first fell in love, Erik? Oh yeah, I remember. She said, 'Take me to California, I want to see the ocean.'

FLO. I want to see the ocean.

RON. As soon as he said yes he knew it was trouble. Right away he could see himself on the streets of Los Angeles without his wallet or maybe even without his pants. As it turned out he got no farther than Utah before he found himself hallooing into culvert openings... Another sunny honeymoon on the dusty road, all on his own with the grasshoppers and the rattlesnakes, still a hundred miles from anywhere. She was beautiful and said all the silly things he wanted to hear.

FLO. Like what?

RON. She said, 'Come with me and you can have your own life.'

FLO. Did she give you your own life?

RON. Sure, sure she did, he spent twenty years sorting other people's mail for the US post office.

Pause.

FLO. Water has come to a halt here in the *lake*. Stymied. All life here eventually ends up as muck under the water. You can reach down and bring up a hundred years in a single handful; the substance of things hoped for.

Pause.

Water does not want to be still. The ocean rages in its bed even though there is nowhere to go. Down, always down. When a fissure opens in the ground water pours in. 'On to the center of the earth!'

Blackout.

Scene Two

Wishing

Lights up.

A few moments later. RON *has disappeared.*

FLO *is reading aloud from* Moby Dick.

ERIK *is fishing.*

FLO. 'All that most maddens and torments; all that stirs up the lees of things; all truth with malice in it; all that cracks the sinews and cakes the brain; all the subtle demonisms of life and thought; all evil, to crazy Ahab, were visibly personified, and made practically assailable in Moby Dick. He piled upon the whale's white hump the sum of all the general rage and hate felt by his whole race from Adam down; and then, as if his chest had been a mortar, he burst his hot heart's shell upon it.'

Now quoting from Moby Dick.

'Towards thee I roll, thou all-destroying but unconquering whale; to the last I grapple with thee; from hell's heart I stab at thee; for hate's sake I spit my last breath at thee. Sink all coffins and all hearses to one common pool! and since neither can be mine, let me then tow to pieces, while still chasing thee, though tied to thee, thou damned whale! Thus, I give up the spear!'

My Grandpa Wayne, he's a spear fisherman. In fact he doesn't even call it fishing. He says it's hunting. He hates fishermen. He got a sturgeon weighing a hundred and four pounds last year, right here where we're sitting. I saw the picture. Sturgeon are bottom feeders, so it's very difficult to spear them. What's this thing?

ERIK. A phosphorescent ice-hole sleeve.

FLO. What's it for?

ERIK. Stop you falling in your ice hole when it's dark.

FLO. You gonna fish till it's dark?

ERIK. Maybe.

FLO. You want to catch a nice fish like that sturgeon?

ERIK. I wish.

FLO. You know, wishes, what people hope for, if they come true, always have a way of turning out badly.

ERIK. You think?

FLO. All the old stories tell you that. The fisherman's wife got wealth and power but wound up with nothing. Tithonus was given eternal life by Zeus but not eternal youth so the gift had unpleasant consequences. King Midas did not do well with his wish either. Captain Ahab, he speared the great white whale he wished for, but he got tangled up in the ropes and he was dragged to the bottom of the sea, so that's not good.

ERIK. You know a lot of stories.

FLO. Not just stories. Suppose I wished to be far away from the stupid repressive town I grew up in and suddenly I was whirled away in a cloud of dust. Before long some well-intentioned fool would miss me and wish me home again. If you wished for a beautiful woman or a rich and handsome husband you *know* what would happen.

ERIK. So, what is there to wish for finally? A blindfold and a last cigarette?

FLO. No, we all know how bad smoking is for our health. I guess, when the genie comes out of the bottle or the man comes to your door with a check the size of a billboard you should say 'No.' 'No thank you.' Say, 'I don't want any.' Say, 'I wish you would go away.'

ERIC. But you aren't going to, are you?

Blackout.

Scene Three

Tumbling

Lights up.

WAYNE *can be seen far in the distance approaching from the shore.*

RON *is back with a propane canister, but has slipped and fallen over.*

FLO. Walking on the ice demands your attention.

RON. You have to learn to read the color, the texture, learn where you can safely step, learn to watch for the smooth, almost invisible ice or ice hidden by a light dusting of snow – suddenly you're flat on your back.

FLO. Yea, if a person of your age falls, it makes a considerable impact. Children don't worry about it. They fall, jump up and continue running. It's nothing. The very old, old men shoveling snow on rooftops, they seem to have forgotten the ice entirely. If they were caught by the least wind their frail bodies would skitter and clatter over the hard surface for miles.

RON. I'm not that old.

FLO. Out on the Great Plains, where I was born, the wind blows constantly. When I was a kid I'd get my allowance and run as hard as I could to the Lotta-Burger or the movie theater only to find it had blown away.

ERIK. What?

FLO. Going home was no better. Sometimes it would take a couple of days to find my house. Under these conditions it was impossible to get acquainted with the neighbors. It was a shock to open the front door and be faced with the county jail, the Pentecostal Church or Aunt Erma carrying two large suitcases. Trash from all over the state caught and piled up at the edge of town and during the windiest times of spring sometimes whole days blew away in a cloud of dust.

RON. Whole days?

FLO. I feel my natural lifespan may have been shortened by the experience. Still, it was a great place to grow up. As the old boy said, 'You can have those big cities, people all jammed together. Give me some wide-open spaces.' Anyway, what I wanted to say, falling is just physics. In the morning out on the plains you have a couple of cups of coffee, get all wound up and go like hell across an open field, try to bounce, clear both ditches and the highway...

RON. The highway?

FLO. Yea, so you don't get caught in the barbed wire, fly from one fenced-in nothing to another, hit the ground and keep on rolling.

ERIK. Keep on rolling.

FLO. Hey, do either of you guys want to try the sauna?

Blackout.

Scene Four

Somersaults

Lights up.

WAYNE *is still approaching, but now nearer.*

Sounds of the lake, snowmobiles, children playing far away, etc.

Smoke comes from the chimney of the sauna house. RON *is inside having a sauna.*

The puppet of FLO *is lying on the sofa reading* Moby Dick.

ERIK. Some children did handsprings or cartwheels. Those of us who were less athletically gifted did what we called somersaults, really a kind of forward roll. Head down in the summer grass. A push with the feet, then the world flipped upside down and around. Your feet, which had been behind you, now stretched out in front. It was fun and we did it, laughing, again and again. Yet, as fun as it was, most of us, at some point, quit doing somersaults. But only recently, someone at Evening Rest (Managed Care for Seniors) discovered the potential value of somersaults as physical and emotional therapy for the aged, a recapturing of youth, perhaps. Every afternoon, weather permitting, the old people, despite their feeble protests, are led or wheeled on to the lawn, where each is personally and individually aided in the heels-over-head tumble into darkness. When the wind is right you can hear, even at this distance, the crying of those who have fallen and are unable to rise.

Blackout.

We only hear what we need of the weather report to cover the scene change.

WEATHER VOICE (DNR MAN). Well, folks, just when you thought the credits were going to roll on this long winter, here we go again, the blizzard of the season looks set to roll in, we're getting reports of seventy-four inches in three hours from some of the outlying areas... it's a white-out, folks...

Tonight we're looking at lake-effect snow showers with thunder and lightning... heavy at times... diminishing into

the morning... expect some blowing and rifting snow...
especially in open areas near Lake Superior... See the latest
Winter Weather message for further details... Weather
spotters are encouraged to submit snowfall reports on our
webpage or through Facebook or Twitter pages. This is
a hazardous weather outlook for portions of...

Scene Five

Old Man Winter

Lights up.

WAYNE *is sitting on* RON*'s bucket with his spear.*

ERIK *is checking the pop-up rig downstage left.* RON *is still having a sauna.*

FLO *still lies reading on the sofa.*

Smoke rises from the chimney of the sauna house.

WAYNE (*speaking with the audience*). Old Man Winter doesn't like anything. He doesn't like dogs or cats or squirrels or birds, especially seagulls, or children or smart-ass college students. He doesn't like loggers or environmentalists or snowmobilers or skiers in their stupid spandex outfits. He doesn't like Christmas or television, or newspapers for that matter. He doesn't like lawyers or politicians. There is a thing or two he could say to the host of the local talk-radio show but he knows for a fact that the son-of-a-bitch does the broadcast from his condo in Florida. He doesn't like foreigners and he doesn't like his neighbors (not that he has many); and when they finally die they just leave their junk all over the yard. He doesn't like that. He doesn't like the look of the sky right now, either, overcast, a kind of jaundice color. He hates that. And that stand of spruce trees behind the house turning black in the dusk... The way it gets dark earlier every day. He doesn't like that.

WAYNE *turns to look at* ERIK.

What are you doing?

ERIK. Fishing.

WAYNE. You call that fishing? With your depth-finders, your underwater cameras, and all your gadgets and gewgaws. You think you know more about what's going on under the ice with all this crap? Give me one good Ojibwa boy, under a deerskin with a spear and nothing but his own two eyes!

ERIK. Spearing is against the law now.

WAYNE. Against the law? There are other laws. Half of you idiots head for home as soon as your radar's out of juice. You wouldn't know a fish nibbling if it pulled you through your hole and kissed you. The fish taught the Ojibwa how to fish. The fish did.

Beat.

Catch anything?

ERIK. Not yet.

WAYNE. Talk to your bait?

ERIK. What?

WAYNE. Have you had words with your lure?

ERIK. Can't say I have.

WAYNE *takes* ERIK's *pole. He holds the bait in the air.*

WAYNE. Son, you got to go down there again. I know it's dark and the water is deep. The ice is all around you, and there's the thinnest line ties you to me. This is the way your life is going to be, out and back, again and again, partly in this world, partly in the other, never at home in either. Still, it's what you were born to do. You are young and strong, all steel and hooks. You know we'll do everything we can to bring you back safely. Get down there, boy, and bring home a big fish for your old father to eat.

There, that'll do it.

You ever seen a dark house?

Blackout.

Scene Six

Ron's Small Park

Lights up.

Late afternoon, approaching sunset.

RON *has come out of the sauna. He stands alone downstage,*
red-faced and steaming, in a bathrobe and head towel. The
puppet of FLO *is now standing next to the sauna house.*
WAYNE *and* ERIK *have gone offstage to visit the dark house.*

RON. You could think of it as a small park. Well, not exactly
a park, a little space between two busy streets, a city
beautification project, an afterthought of city planners, all
nicely bricked, with a park bench and an old maple tree that
predates any planning, nothing else. It's a space nobody uses,
really. Nobody sits on the bench. The drunks throw empty
wine bottles here, now and then. And occasionally a bird,
a crow or a sparrow lands on a bare branch of the tree, on its
way elsewhere. You could think of the leaves that have fallen
as all of your dreams and hopes that have fallen and blown
away. But there is no park really, and no bare branch where
a bird could land. There is only this empty space that you
cherish and protect, where once your heart was.

Blackout.

Scene Seven

Bowling

WAYNE *and* ERIK *are walking back from the dark house.*

ERIK *is holding a bowling pin.* WAYNE *is still holding his spear.*

FLO *has gone inside the sauna house to change her clothes.*

RON *is where he was, getting dressed.*

WAYNE. I heard a jack fish scream once off the coast of Africa. Cried like a baby in the bottom of the boat.

ERIK. Africa?

WAYNE. I was on safari. Big game hunting. Trophies. The sound of a thing dying can get to you, but it's the eyes you never forget. Most hunters wait for the animal to die before getting close. A quarter of a million deer shot each year in Minnesota. How many do you think see their killer? I betcha ten, tops. I've seen grown men walk out of the woods and never come back just because they looked in those deep-brown, eyelashed eyes... But, ah, cripes, they'd do the same to us if they could.

ERIK. Deer?

WAYNE. No, big game. Lions, alligators, Hippopotamus are the worst. It just depends where you happen to be in the food chain. Mushrooms will eat up a plate of Alaskan crude oil, who's to say they wouldn't eat us if we lay still long enough.

ERIK. That would be a slow death.

WAYNE. I can think of worse.

ERIK. I used to hunt mushrooms, with my dad. He used to get real angry because they were never where he said they would be. Just when he thought he knew something, when he thought he had discerned some pattern, a certain strategy – ah, they grow on the north edge of the low mossy spots – I would find one on top of a rise and it would shoot his theory all to shit.

WAYNE. The truth is there is no thought that goes into this. These things just pop up. And all this thinking, this human consciousness, isn't what it's cracked up to be. He was just pissed off because you're a natural hunter.

ERIK. He was pissed off about more than that. The best anyone can say about you is that you are a disappointment. We had higher expectations of you. We had hoped that you would finish your schooling. We had hoped that you would have kept your job at the plant. We had hoped that you would have been a better son and a better father. We hoped, and fully expected, that you would finish reading *Moby Dick*. I wish that, when I am talking to you, you would at least raise your head off your desk and look at me. There are people who, without your gifts, have accomplished so much in this life. I am truly disappointed. Your parents, your wife and children, your entire family, in fact, everyone you know is disappointed, deeply disappointed.

WAYNE. Mushrooms grow in the dark. What do you want?

ERIK. This is Ron, Ron Ganzer, this is Wayne Johnson.

RON. What's with the spear?

ERIK. He's a spear fisherman.

WAYNE. Hunter.

ERIK. He gave me this decoy.

RON. Looks like a bowling pin.

ERIK. He uses it as a decoy, to lure the fish.

RON. Why would a fish believe a bowling pin is something it could eat?

ERIK. We all have certain things we believe in. Usually they don't amount to much.

WAYNE. All you have to do is get the big fish close enough to spear him. By the time he sees it's a bowling pin he's chewing on steel.

RON. I guess it's best to keep your distance when you find yourself believing in bowling pins.

WAYNE. Originally, bowling was a part of German religious ceremonies. Bowling pins were something that parishioners carried around for protection, like a cudgel or a bludgeon. The church told them if they stood their cudgel up at the end of a long lane and knocked it over with a rolling rock, their sins would be absolved. Martin Luther had a couple of lanes in his back yard.

The puppet of FLO *appears at the window of the sauna house.*

RON. Flo asked me to get the barbecue going before it's too dark.

ERIK. We're not staying for dinner.

WAYNE. Ice fish have to be eaten raw, like sushi. If you cook an ice fish you wind up with nothing but a skillet full of water. Gnash one down or swallow it whole, there is nothing like the flavor, full of the glittering, bitter cold of a January day. Your teeth crack, your tongue goes numb, your lips turn blue, and your eyes roll back in your head. 'God,' you say, 'God that was good! Let me have just one more.'

Blackout.

Scene Eight

Who Aren't We?

Lights up.

Sunset.

FLO is dressed in a vintage spring dress with a man's hat, a pipe and jacket.

She is tending the barbecue, which is full size and has been lit.

There is also a full-size cooler and a camera on a tripod.

ERIK and RON are packing up their stuff to leave.

WAYNE is sitting.

Behind them the sauna house is lit with a smaller fiber-optic palm tree and fairy lights.

FLO. Spring's just around the corner! Can't you feel it? Seagulls sailing close to the wind, clouds running before, everything moving, the waves breaking on some far shore and the water here, right where we're standing, all rippled and nervous, the sun stirring the wind which has pushed the ice far out into the lake, the sun itself comes spinning in from deep space, the snow melting, pussy willows and catkins, marsh marigolds in the ditch,

RON. leaves turning green again,

FLO. everything wanting and growing.

RON. Spring. It seems to indicate... something. But what?

FLO. There is no one to ask. No one and nothing has any more idea what's going on than you do.

ERIK. When one is young every day (as I remember it) is the first day of spring, all headlong and heedless. But, it turns out that life really is short and before you know it you are old and filled with sadness. Nothing to do now but watch the birds, scratch a few petroglyphs for someone to puzzle over years from now, to stay out of the way and leave the bulk of the wanton destruction to those who are younger. The human race will evolve or go extinct. So what?

WAYNE. Yeah, So what? It happens all the time. You never see saber-toothed tigers anymore. I suppose I should be sorry about that, but to tell the truth I never liked them. All that screaming and prowling around outside the house at night – who needs it?

FLO. The colors of that sunset are amazing! You know I see people as colors. My friend Jenny is yellow or gold.

RON. Because she is blond?

FLO. No it's not that. I think of Erik, for instance, as black, like a pirate flag, but his hair is quite blond.

ERIK. Ron, come on, we've got to go, keep packing up.

RON. Yeah. What color are you?

FLO. Oh, I'm spring colors; maybe that bright green that you see when the leaves are still small. (Kind of young and dumb.)

RON. What about me? What color am I?

FLO. Oh, I see you as brown.

RON. Brown.

FLO. Shades of brown.

ERIK. Ron.

RON. Yeah. Why are you all dressed up like that?

FLO. I decided that it would be nice to be someone else for a change. I call myself Art. Being someone else is kind of like having a guest, so my job is to make Art feel welcome and happy. What would Art like? Art would like coffee, I think, so off I go. When I meet someone I say 'How do you do? Name's Art.'

RON. But your name is Flo, not Art.

WAYNE. You've always been Flo.

FLO. Oh, all right then, call me Flo. You see, Art is a very easy-going guy. I just don't see why people have to be so inflexible, so unequivocal, so… definite. Meanwhile, I have learned that Art likes to wear a dress, and smoke a pipe while

he thinks about theoretical physics. Yes, I think that's what
Art feels like. Me too.

*Two or three snowmobiles roar by quite near, with people
shouting or loud music playing if need be.*

WAYNE. When we moved out here thirty years ago there
weren't so many paved roads. There were fewer houses,
fewer people. There weren't so many lights. Could be there's
more of everything now. It seems to me we get more snow
now than we used to.

We were a long way from town in those days but we didn't see
so many animals. There were tracks, only suggestions... I'm
sure we see more moose nowadays. It was quiet. There was
the wind in the spruce trees that seemed sometimes as if it
were saying something, but wasn't. Often on clear nights
you'd see the aurora. Basically, though, there was nothing out
here. That's changed. It's hard to explain the way things used
to be. It's hard to find words to explain the loss of nothing.

RON. It isn't so much because of the desire for what has been
lost, as it is the loss of desire itself, that I stand here, like a
child whose big rubber ball has washed out to sea, on the
verge of tears.

Gunshots ring out from far away across the lake.

*The sunset is at its most beautiful, changing. The lake
booms.*

*The wind carries sounds from the shore; occasional
gunshots, moose calls, music.*

WAYNE *walks forward.*

WAYNE. Hunting season, bullets flying everywhere. Best to
sing or shout as you go along.

ERIK. Ron, it's getting dark.

FLO (*sings*).
    The sweetest songs belong to lovers in the gloaming,
    The sweetest days are days that used to be.
    The saddest words I ever heard were words of parting
    When you said 'Sweetheart, remember me.'

> Remember me when the candle lights are gleaming,
> Remember me at the close of a long long day.
> It would be so sweet when all alone I'm dreaming.
> Just to know you still remember me.

More gunshots ring out from far away across the lake.

RON *and* ERIK *sing along.*

> Remember me when the candle lights are gleaming,
> Remember me at the close of a long long day.
> It would be so sweet when all alone I'm dreaming.
> Just to know you still remember me.

WAYNE. At dusk the light chooses carefully the things it loves; the water, the white belly of the fish, the hands of the fisherman, the bright blade of the knife.

Over there one shaft of sunlight *penetrating* the clouds as if it were an indicator: the finger of God pointing out... something. As if something was being called to my attention What is it, Lord? More frozen trees? What is it? It's as if someone leaving on a train says something as the cars begin to move, something through the glass. I can see his lips moving. Gestures. What? I can't hear you. What?

Blackout.

Scene Nine

A Bazillion Stars Overhead

An hour later.

Darkness.

The stars are out.

There are lights on the distant shore including a distant lighthouse.

The sofa and fiber-optic tree which were next to the sauna house are now downstage and full scale.

FLO, WAYNE, ERIK *and* RON *are finishing dinner.*

At some point FLO *fetches some battery lanterns from* ERIK'*s equipment for light.*

The barbecue gives off a red glow when anyone stands or sits near it.

RON. Don't talk to me about allergies. My family. Lyle can't eat any onions or garlic. Ann can only eat onions if they are well cooked and cut into tiny pieces. Jim is extremely allergic to nuts. Phil is allergic to shellfish. Steve has a violent reaction to celery. Patricia is allergic to beef. Connie cannot eat processed meat. No fat for Joe. Dennis cannot eat any spicy food. Frank believes he is allergic to vinegar. Georganne is unable to tolerate mayonnaise. Michael is allergic to eggs and certain fish. Charlie and Sue do not eat meat, except fish. Thomas will eat no vegetables and no fish… 'Ick!' Dylan eats no meat or dairy products, except once when he ate an entire large cheese pizza. Peter will not eat cheese. Richard won't eat anything. Almost no one drinks anymore except Walt who drinks too much and has to be sent home in a taxi. Elaine cannot stand Caroline so they have to be seated at opposite ends of the table. More, anyone?

FLO. Hey, look at the train.

They hear a train passing along the shore and also see a plane flying across the sky. While the others turn to watch, ERIK *speaks with the audience.*

ERIK. At first I refused to deliver junk mail because it was
stupid, all those deodorant ads, money-making ideas and
contests. Then I began to doubt the importance of the other
mail I carried. I began to randomly select first class mail for
non-delivery. After I had finished my mail route each day
I would return home with a handful of letters and put them
in the attic. I didn't open them and never even looked at
them again. It was as if I were an agent of Fate, capricious
and blind. In the several years before I was caught, friends
vanished, marriages failed, business deals fell through.
Toward the end I became more and more bold, deleting
houses, then whole blocks from my route. I began to feel I'd
been born in the wrong era. If only I could have been a Pony
Express rider galloping into some prairie town with an
empty bag, or the runner from Marathon collapsing in the
streets of Athens, gasping, 'No news.'

FLO. Room for salad, anyone? I've got Glorified Rice, cookie
salad, Jell-O salad or Snickers salad.

RON. No thanks. I'm fine.

ERIK. One day you cross an invisible line and everything is
changed. But what? It is as if you had crossed the
international dateline, all at once it's another day. Now,
everything you looked forward to is suddenly behind.

FLO. But all those things that have gone from your life, moon
boots, TV trays and the Soviet Union, that seem to have
vanished, are really only changed, dinosaurs did not
disappear from the earth but evolved into birds... Crock-Pots
became bread-makers... and then the bread-makers all went
to rummage sales along with the exercise bikes.

RON. Everything around you changes.

ERIK. Nothing is the same as it used to be.

FLO. Except us, of course, we haven't changed... we're the same
as ever, constant in our instability. Look, a bazillion stars
overhead and I look up as amazed and baffled as the first
hominid who gazed upward must have been, stars passing
overhead like a very slow-moving flock of birds, going
somewhere, disappearing into the wee hours of the morning.

RON. I used to be able to recognize some of the constellations; the Pleiades, the Big Dipper... but I have forgotten most.

FLO. Still, mankind has learned a lot about the cosmos since Galileo's time.

RON. A friend of mine, *his* wife bought *him* a telescope for *his* birthday, a nice one, very powerful. *He's* got it set up on the deck. You know, when you look at a star with your naked eye all you see is a little white dot, but when you look at it through a telescope you see a bigger white dot.

FLO. The moon looks worried, rising above the lake. The moon looks so unhappy, so pale. The moon has not been well. The moon has had a lot of problems with meteors, especially in youth. And night after night, the same earth rises... It hasn't been easy for the moon. The moon... The moon... The moon this and the moon that. You drive faster but the moon keeps pace, looking sadly into your car window. 'Why are you leaving,' the moon wonders, 'and where will you go?'

ERIK. Feels like it might snow later.

RON. Yea soon it'll be November again and the snow will come sudden and heavy.

ERIK. This is what we like best.

RON. This is what we paid our money for.

ERIK. Snow on snow, all day and all night,

RON. everything muffled,

ERIK. distant.

RON. Tomorrow, no school,

ERIK. no work,

RON. no worship service,

ERIK. no visitation of the sick, the poor,

RON. the widows or the orphans.

ERIK. Whatever it was nothing can be done about it now.

RON. Your old position has been filled.

ERIK. Your footsteps have been filled.

RON. The roads are filled,

ERIK. drifted shut.

RON. Finally, even the directions are obliterated in the heavy snowfall.

ERIK. And you missed your turn two miles back because you weren't paying attention:

RON. daydreaming.

ERIK. So now you have decided to turn here,

RON. on the wrong road,

ERIK. just because you are too lazy to turn around.

RON. You have decided to turn here just because of some vague notion.

ERIK. You have decided to turn here just because you aren't smart enough not to.

RON. You have decided to turn here... just because.

ERIK. You have decided to turn here... just because.

FLO. Listen, help is available. There are people who have experience with this kind of thing, people who have been through this. There are hotlines. There are brochures.

There are programs, support groups. There is financial aid. Listen. The angels gather around you like gnats, strumming their guitars, singing songs of salvation, singing songs of freedom and diversity.

RON. But you aren't listening.

ERIK. We aren't listening.

RON. Here we are on the genuine road less traveled.

ERIK. The road never snowplowed.

RON. Nothing to do but follow the ruts.

ERIK. Nothing to do but follow the ruts.

RON. Here the snow is too deep to turn around.

ERIK. We are going to have to follow this road to whatever nowhere it leads to.

WAYNE. We die of silliness, finally. Remember all those nights of wine, the heated discussion, the smoky room, the music? Those questions you pondered then have no relevance. 'Why do we live?' you asked. More to the point now is, 'Where do I live?' First you forget to zip then; as time goes by you forget to unzip. There is a banana peel around every corner. Remember all those powerful, intense things you said back then, how the girls found you powerful and intense? You couldn't say those things with a straight face now, and anyway, those girls weren't really listening. The old lion, with patchy mane and sagging belly stands up to guard his territory. He gives a pathetic roar and the hyenas die laughing.

FLO *has one of the torches.*

FLO. The only light is the light you carry. You can feel the darkness coming up close behind. If you turn suddenly the darkness jumps back, the way the lion retreats momentarily from the desperate wildebeest.

Once you were a beacon. Once you set the candlestick atop your head and did the rumba, the cha-cha, the limbo, until the wee hours of the morning.

You hold that candle so carefully in front of you that it makes strange shadows and lines across your face but, honestly, I've never seen you looking better. We should take a picture! Closer, closer, guys.

FLO *encourages them all to pose for the camera.*

There is only, as there always was, the moment. The instant, which, when you become aware of it, is blinding as the flash when someone snaps a picture of you blowing out the candles. Hold still. Smile, fellas.

As FLO *takes the picture, there is a distant sound of ice booming and a flash.*

While the men focus on the camera, FLO *speaks directly with the audience.*

Do you know, at our house, it turns out that the drainpipe from the sink is attached to nothing and water just runs right on to the ground in the crawl space underneath the house and then trickles out into the stream that passes through the back yard.

Another distant sound of ice booming and groaning.

It turns out that the house is not really attached to the ground but sits atop a few loose concrete blocks all held in place by gravity, which, as I understand it, means 'seriousness'. Well, this is serious enough. If you look into it further you will discover that the water is not attached to anything either and that perhaps the rocks and the trees are not all that firmly in place.

FLO *jumps or steps or lets herself down off the ice-lake stage on to the theater's stage floor.*

The world is a stage. But don't try to move anything. You might hurt yourself, besides that's a job for the stagehands and union rules are strict.

The crew come on and strike everything to do with WAYNE *and* FLO, *except the fiber-optic palm tree and the bowling pin. The barbecue, the cooler, the sofa, the sauna house and the other miniature ice houses, are all struck.*

FLO *beckons for* WAYNE *to join her, which he does, stepping off the ice on to the stage floor. She still has the torch.*

You are merely a player about to deliver a soliloquy on the septic system to a couple dozen popple trees and a patch of dark-blue sky.

There is a frightening sound of ice breaking and shifting.

ERIK *and* RON *fall over.* WAYNE *and* FLO *take seats in the house to watch the rest of the play.*

ACT THREE

Scene One

Where's the Edge?

The ice they are on has broken off from the shore and is floating out into the lake.

Nothing remains except the fiber-optic palm tree, and the men's fishing equipment, which has been cleared to the side.

The shoreline in the distance is bobbing up and down as if the ice they are on is rocking. If possible the shoreline moves from one side to the other before disappearing.

The scene begins while the crew are still clearing.

RON. She's gone.

   He's gone.

   They've gone.

ERIK. The ice is moving.

RON. The ice is moving and they've gone.

ERIK. We've broken off.

RON. Where's the land, Erik?

ERIK. It's over there.

RON. It's going up and down.

ERIK. We're going up and down. We're drifting out.

RON. This is out of control.

ERIK. We're floating out into the lake.

RON. What are we going to do, Erik?

ERIK. We've still got the truck.

RON. Where's the edge?

ERIK. I've got my phone.

RON. For God's sake, call someone.

ERIK *is holding his cellphone.*

RON *stands at the back of the stage and touches the hanging stars.*

ERIK. Insects never worry about where they are. A mosquito is so dedicated to the pursuit of warm blood that it neglects the long-range plan. If a mosquito follows you into the house it waits patiently until the lights are out and you are nearly asleep and then it heads straight for your ear. Suppose you miss, hit yourself in the head and knock yourself out and the mosquito succeeds in drawing blood. How will it get out of the house again to breed? What are its chances? Insects don't seem to have a sense of place but require only a certain ambiance. A fly that gets driven five hundred miles in a car and then is finally chased out the window does not miss the town where it spent its maggothood. Wherever this is it will be the same; a pile of dogshit, a tuna-salad sandwich, a corpse.

RON. Hey, Erik, did you make that call yet?

Pause.

Erik!

ERIK. Yeah. In a minute.

RON. In Sitka, because they are fond of them, people have named the sea lions. Every sea lion is named Earl because they are killed one after another by the orca, the killer whale; bodies tossed left and right into the air. 'At least he didn't get Earl,' someone says. And sure enough, after a time, that same friendly, bewhiskered face bobs to the surface. It's Earl again. Well, how else are you to live except by denial, by some palatable fiction, some little song to sing while the inevitable, the black-and-white blindsiding fact, comes hurtling toward you out of the deep?

ERIK. I found the edge, Ron. I found the edge.

A cellphone rings from the downstage-right fishing hole.

RON *goes down and puts his head in the fishing hole.*

ERIK *looks at him.*

The water goes on and on, babbling and blathering about something, something it knows nothing about. It is like listening from your bed as a child to the *ha-ha mumble murmur* of adults in the other room. If you listen the way you did then the water, as well, will put you to sleep. The water says *everything goes, down, down soon everything that happened will not have happened it has been a very long time since you checked the oil in your car a long time since you called your mother everything you used think was important wasn't important what you were told was important wasn't what you think is important now isn't important only what you think is unimportant only what you did not even think of only what you could never think of could never imagine is important... but not very important...*

Scene Two

I Don't Belong Here

The DNR MAN*'s head appears out of the ice hole* RON *has been looking into. He proceeds to climb out and sit on the ice.*

ERIK *has turned upstage to look at the stars.*

DNR. 'I don't belong here,' I tell myself over and over. 'I was never good at swimming and I have no sense of direction.' Once again I was lost and couldn't find the opening. I managed to breathe by sticking my nose into the little pockets of air just beneath the ice, gasping... Then suddenly, by some miracle, over here, not fifty feet away, the light shining down from the other world. I haul my ass out on to the ice sheet. At last. I can warm my blubber in the sunshine, have a cup of coffee, some orange juice, maybe have one or two of those little almond cookies, read a bit of the newspaper, find out what's happening in New York and Los Angeles, maybe even smoke a cigar before I'm noticed.

He discovers RON*'s phone in his pocket.*

In the old days telephones were made of *whale vertebrae* and were big and heavy enough to be used to fight off an intruder. The telephone had a special place in the front hallway, a shrine built into the wall, a niche previously occupied by the blessed virgin.

Nowadays telephones are made of recycled plastic bags and have multiplied to the point where they have become a major nuisance. The phone might ring at you from anywhere; the car, the bathroom, out of your coat pocket in a silent darkened theater... Everyone hates the telephone. No one uses the telephone anymore so telephones, out of habit or boredom or loneliness perhaps, call one another. 'Please leave a message at the tone.' 'I'm sorry, this is a courtesy call. We'll call back at a more convenient time. There is no message.'

He gives the phone back to RON.

By the way, this is not the end, but you can see the end from here. Well, often when you think you have come to the end

there is one more thing. Out there is a scattering of islands
some thick with spruce and balsam, *frozen* marshes and
bogs. Easy to get bogged down with last-minute details. It's
better to think of each island as a stepping-stone. Flag Island,
South Government, North Government, Merritt Island, and
last of all Passage Island with its light, not the light at the
end of the tunnel, not the warm encompassing light, just a
brief flash and then... it comes again. Beyond all are the
open waters of the big lake... Each passenger receives a hug,
a bouquet of flowers, a small box of candy.

Scene Three

Nice Fish

The downstage tip-up's flag flips up.

The DNR MAN *drops down his hole again.*

ERIK *goes to check the flag.*

ERIK *pulls a beautiful fish from the hole.* RON *watching.*

RON. When he finally landed the fish it seemed so strange, so unlike other fishes he'd caught, so much bigger, more silvery,

ERIK. more important,

RON. that he half-expected it to talk, to grant his wishes if he returned it to the water.

ERIK. But the fish said nothing, made no pleas, gave no promises. His fishing partner said,

RON. 'Nice fish, you ought to have it mounted.' Other people who saw it said the same thing.

RON *and* ERIK. 'Nice fish...'

RON. So he took it to the taxidermy shop but when it came back it didn't look quite the same.

ERIK. Still, it was an impressive trophy.

RON. Mounted on a big board the way it was, it was too big to fit in the car. In those days he could fit everything he owned into the back of his Volkswagen but the fish changed all that. After he married, a year or so later, nothing would fit in the car. He got a bigger car. Then a new job, children...

ERIK. The fish moved with them from house to house, state to state.

RON. All that moving around took its toll on the fish, it began to look worn, a fin was broken off. It went into the attic of the new house. Just before the divorce became final, when he was moving to an apartment, his wife said,

ERIK. 'Take your goddamn fish.'

RON. He hung the fish on the wall before he'd unpacked anything else. The fish seemed huge, too big for his little apartment.

ERIK. Boy, it was big.

RON. He couldn't imagine he'd ever caught a fish that big.

ERIK *returns the fish down the ice hole.*

Snow begins falling heavily all over the stage if possible.

They take shelter under the fiber-optic tree with the bowling pin.

ERIK. You look for deeper meanings in things.

RON. There are signs and portents, though sometimes you deny it.

ERIK. You find special significance in certain places and days,

RON. the cottage by the lake,

ERIK. Christmas,

RON. a certain Chinese restaurant in Winnipeg,

ERIK. your birthday.

RON. You set them up like signposts marking the passage of your life.

ERIK. One after another they multiply until you're surrounded by a forest of sticks.

RON. Jackstraws.

ERIK. Touch one and they all fall down.

RON. Jack Straw,

ERIK. head full of hay,

RON. reading long boring books,

ERIK. waiting for the mail,

RON. watching the days go by.

*There is a flash of lightning in the snowy sky creating
a complete*

White-out.

*Then, a few moments later, there is a deep boom of thunder
in the distance.*

ERIK. Here it is Sunday morning

RON. and there's no one downtown but the looney

ERIK. and dysfunctional.

RON. There's old One-Eye who recently returned from Jupiter,

ERIK. and the spooky Woman in White,

RON. Tom Drooley,

ERIK. Mr Ozone Peepot,

RON. Euclid and The Motorcycle Queen,

ERIK. Mr Occupant,

RON. Goofy Walker,

ERIK. Old Man Winter,

RON. still wearing his old winter coat.

ERIK *and* RON. It's spring.

WAYNE. It's April Fools'.

FLO. It's the Easter Parade!

ERIK *and* RON. Grab your hat and let's get in line!

*RON and ERIK take off their boots and jackets, pick up the
hand-held auger and bowling pin, and pretend to march
across the stage in an Easter Parade.*

*There is another flash of lightning in the snowy sky creating
a complete*

White-out.

*Then again there is a deep boom of thunder closer than
before.*

RON *and* ERIK *take off their remaining fishing clothing to reveal white shirts, ties and slacks.*

Hands appear in the ice-fishing holes, holding two clipboards, with clip-on nametags and pencils. RON *and* ERIK *pick them up.*

RON. The speaker points out that we don't really have much of a grasp of things, not only the big things, the important questions, but the small everyday things.

ERIK. How many steps up to your front door?

RON. What kind of tree grows in your back yard?

ERIK. What is the name of your district representative?

RON. What is your wife's shoe size?

ERIK. Can you tell me the color of your sweetheart's eyes?

RON. Do you remember where you parked the car?

They look at each other.

ERIK. The evidence is overwhelming.

RON. Most of us never truly experience life.

They read something the speaker has written on a white board.

ERIK. 'We drift through life in a daydream,

RON. missing the true richness and joy that life has to offer.'

They put down their clipboards.

When the speaker has finished we gather around to sing a few inspirational songs.

ERIK. You and I stand at the back of the group and hum along... since we have forgotten most of the words.

There is a final flash of lightning in the snowy sky creating a complete

White-out.

And a deep boom of thunder is heard directly overhead.

They help to undress each other, aging as they do so, take hands like an old couple and, supporting each other tenderly, take a short walk. RON *wears a slip,* ERIK, *old man pants and vest.*

RON. Old people are exiting this life as if it were a movie...

RON *and* ERIK. 'I didn't get it.'

ERIK. 'It didn't seem to have any plot.'

RON. 'No.' she says, 'it seemed like things just kept coming at me. Most of the time I was confused... and there was way too much sex and violence.'

ERIK. 'Violence anyway,' he says.

RON. 'It was not much for character development either; most of the time people were either shouting or mumbling. Then just when someone started to make sense and I got interested, they died. Then a whole lot of new characters came along and I couldn't tell who was who.'

ERIK. 'The whole thing lacked subtlety.'

They walk under the fiber-optic tree.

RON. 'Some of the scenery was nice.'

ERIK. 'Yes.' They walk in silence for a while. It is a summer night and they walk slowly, stopping now and then, as if they had no particular place to go. They walk past a street lamp where some insects are hurling themselves at the light, and then on down the block, fading into the darkness.

Two large fishing lures lower into the space.

RON. She says, 'I was never happy with the way I looked.'

ERIK. 'The lighting was bad and I was no good at dialogue,' he says.

RON. 'I would have liked to have been a little taller,' she says.

Having both got hold of one of the lures, RON *and* ERIK *are lifted into the sky.*

We hear 'Home' played by Coleman Hawkins.

The End.